W9-BIQ-880

DATE DUE

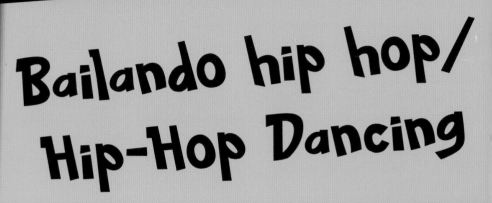

Baila, baila, baila/Dance, Dance, Dance

Bailando hip hop/ Hip-Hop Dancing

por/by Kathryn Clay

Editora consultora/Consulting Editor: Gail Saunders-Smith, PhD

Asesora de contenido/Content Consultant: Heidi L. Schimpf
Directora de Programas y Servicios/Director of Programs and Services
Joy of Motion Dance Center, Washington, D.C.

CAPSTONE PRESS
a capstone imprint

Pebble Plus is published by Capstone Press,
151 Good Counsel Drive, P.O. Box 669, Mankato, Minnesota 56002.
www.capstonepub.com

Books published by Capstone Press are manufactured with paper
containing at least 10 percent post-consumer waste.

Library of Congress Cataloging-in-Publication Data
Clay, Kathryn.
    [Hip-hop dancing. Spanish & English]
    Bailando hip hop / por Kathryn Clay = Hip-hop dancing / by Kathryn Clay.
    p. cm.—(Pebble Plus bilingüe/bilingual. Baila, baila, baila/Dance, dance, dance)
    Includes index.
    Summary: "Simple text and photographs present hip-hop dancing, including simple
steps—in both English and Spanish"—Provided by publisher.
    ISBN 978-1-4296-5351-0 (library binding)
    1. Hip-hop dance—Juvenile literature. I. Title. II. Title: Hip-hop dancing. III. Series.
GV1796.H57C5718 2011
793.3—dc22   2010004184

Editorial Credits
Jennifer Besel, editor; Strictly Spanish, translation services; Veronica Bianchini, set designer;
    Eric Manske and Danielle Ceminsky, designers; Marcie Spence, media researcher;
    Sarah Schuette, photo stylist; Marcy Morin, scheduler; Laura Manthe, production specialist

Photo Credits
All photos by Capstone Studio/Karon Dubke

The Capstone Press Photo Studio thanks Dance Express in
Mankato, Minnesota, and The Dance Connection in Rosemount,
Minnesota, for their help with photo shoots for this book.

Printed in the United States of America in North Mankato, Minnesota.
012011   006047R

Note to Parents and Teachers

The Baila, baila, baila/Dance, Dance, Dance series supports national physical education
standards and the national standards for learning and teaching dance in the arts. This book
describes and illustrates hip-hop dancing in both English and Spanish. The images support early
readers in understanding the text. The repetition of words and phrases helps early readers learn
new words. This book also introduces early readers to subject-specific vocabulary words, which
are defined in the Glossary section. Early readers may need assistance to read some words and
to use the Table of Contents, Glossary, Internet Sites, and Index sections of the book.

Table of Contents

Tabla de contenidos

All about Hip-Hop

Drop to the floor, and pop
back up. Hip-hop dance
is full of energy.

Todo sobre el hip hop

Tírate al piso y párate
rápidamente. El baile hip hop
está lleno de energía.

Hip-hop dancers move
to hip-hop music.
Hip-hop music mixes rap
and fast beats.

Los bailarines de hip hop se
mueven al ritmo de la música
hip hop. La música hip hop
mezcla rap y tiempos rápidos.

What to Wear

Hip-hop dancers wear T-shirts, baggy pants, and shorts. Loose clothing makes it easy to move.

Qué ropa usar

Los bailarines de hip hop usan camisetas, pantalones sueltos y shorts. La ropa suelta facilita el movimiento.

Hip-hop dancers wear sneakers.
Sneakers keep dancers
from slipping on the floor.

Los bailarines de hip hop usan
zapatillas. Las zapatillas
previenen que los bailarines
se resbalen en el piso.

Sweet Steps

Take a step to the right with your right foot. Slide your left toes on the floor to meet your right foot. This move is called a toe drag.

Pasos dulces

Da un paso a la derecha con tu pie derecho. Desliza los dedos de tu pie izquierdo por el suelo hasta tocar tu pie derecho. Este movimiento se llama *toe drag*.

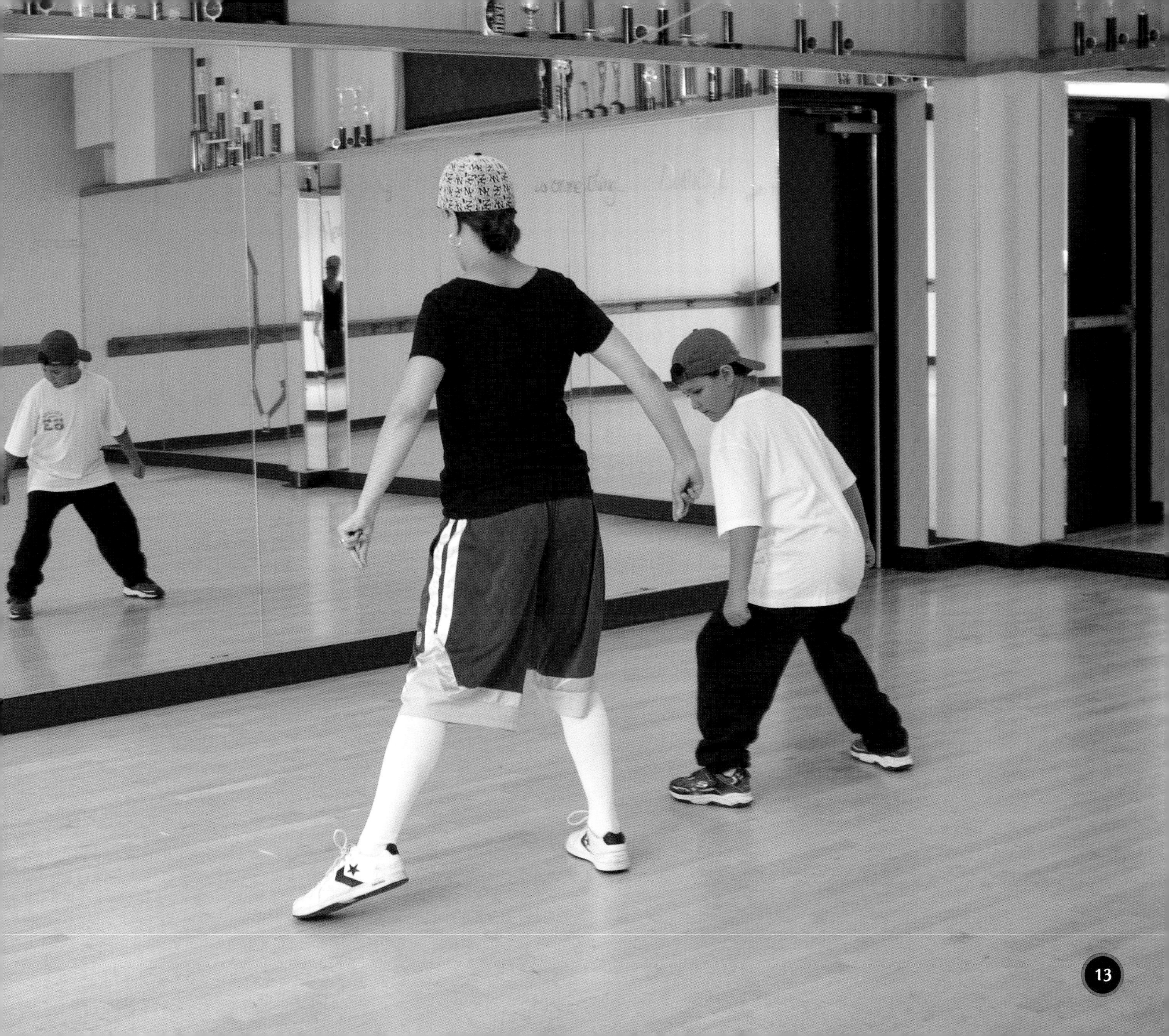

Pull your elbows up
to your sides and freeze.
This move is called locking.

Eleva tus codos a los costados
de tu cuerpo y quédate quieto.
Este movimiento se llama *locking*.

Point one foot in front of you.

Rock your body back and forth.

This move is called top rocking.

Pon un pie en punta enfrente tuyo.

Balancea tu cuerpo hacia adelante y

hacia atrás. Este movimiento

se llama *top rocking*.

Drop down like you're doing a push-up. Then kick your legs wide. This move is called the drop and kick out.

Vete al piso como si fueras a flexionar los brazos. Luego abre tus piernas bien ancho. Este movimiento se llama *drop* y *kick out*.

Ready to Dance

Lock, rock, and

show off your moves.

You're hip-hop dancing!

Listos para bailar

Lock, rock y muestra

tus movimientos.

¡Estás bailando hip hop!

Glossary

baggy—hanging loosely

beat—the rhythm of a piece of music

freeze—to hold still

rap—a type of song in which the words are spoken to the music

Internet Sites

FactHound offers a safe, fun way to find Internet sites related to this book. All of the sites on FactHound have been researched by our staff.

Here's all you do:

Visit *www.facthound.com*

Type in this code: 9781429653510

Glosario

quieto—sin moverse

el rap—un tipo de canción en la que las palabras son habladas al ritmo de la música

suelto—que cuelga sin apretar

el tiempo—el ritmo de una pieza de música

Sitios de Internet

FactHound brinda una forma segura y divertida de encontrar sitios de Internet relacionados con este libro. Todos los sitios en FactHound han sido investigados por nuestro personal.

Esto es todo lo que tienes que hacer:

Visita *www.facthound.com*

Ingresa este código: 9781429653510

Index

Índice